smart girl's GUIDE

RACE & INCLUSION

standing up to racism and building a better world

by Deanna Singh
illustrated by Shellene Rodney

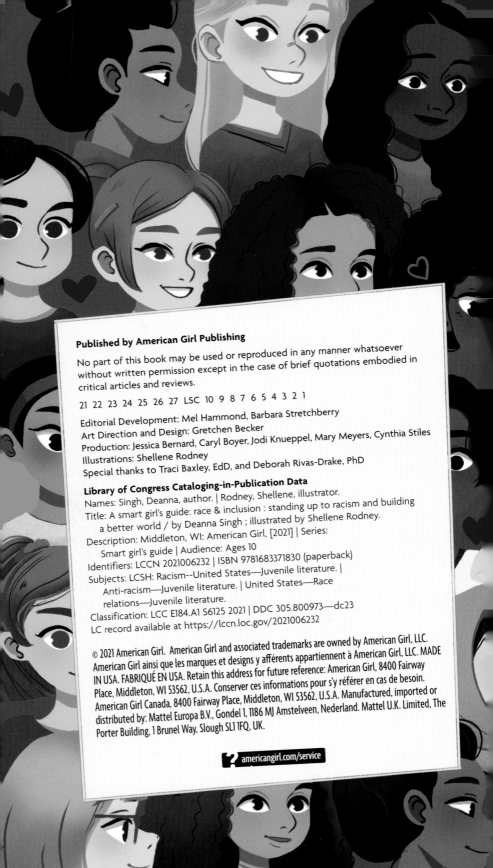

Published by American Girl Publishing

21 22 23 24 25 26 27 LSC 10 9 8 7 6 5 4 3 2 1

Editorial Development: Mel Hammond, Barbara Stretchberry
Art Direction and Design: Gretchen Becker
Production: Jessica Bernard, Caryl Boyer, Jodi Knueppel, Mary Meyers, Cynthia Stiles
Illustrations: Shellene Rodney
Special thanks to Traci Baxley, EdD, and Deborah Rivas-Drake, PhD

Library of Congress Cataloging-in-Publication Data
Names: Singh, Deanna, author. | Rodney, Shellene, illustrator.
Title: A smart girl's guide: race & inclusion : standing up to racism and building
    a better world / by Deanna Singh ; illustrated by Shellene Rodney.
Description: Middleton, WI: American Girl, [2021] | Series:
    Smart girl's guide | Audience: Ages 10
Identifiers: LCCN 2021006232 | ISBN 9781683371830 (paperback)
Subjects: LCSH: Racism--United States—Juvenile literature. |
    Anti-racism—Juvenile literature. | United States—Race
    relations—Juvenile literature.
Classification: LCC E184.A1 S6125 2021 | DDC 305.800973—dc23
LC record available at https://lccn.loc.gov/2021006232

americangirl.com/service

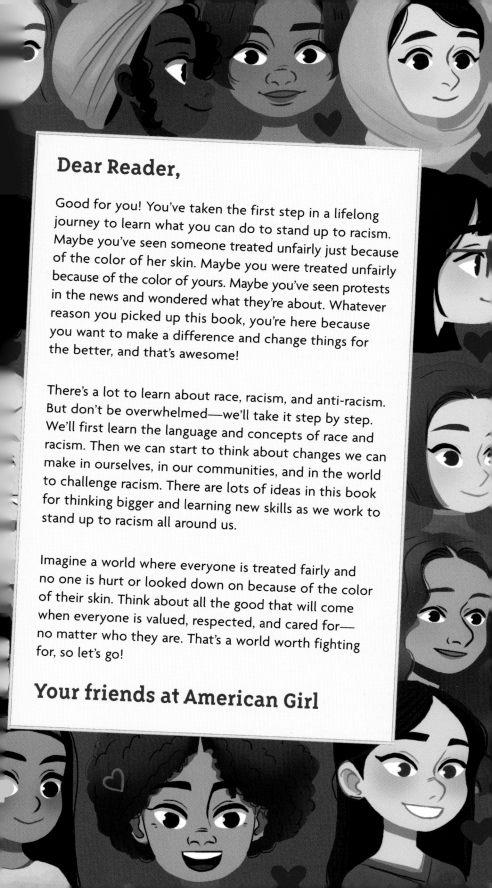

Dear Reader,

Good for you! You've taken the first step in a lifelong journey to learn what you can do to stand up to racism. Maybe you've seen someone treated unfairly just because of the color of her skin. Maybe you were treated unfairly because of the color of yours. Maybe you've seen protests in the news and wondered what they're about. Whatever reason you picked up this book, you're here because you want to make a difference and change things for the better, and that's awesome!

There's a lot to learn about race, racism, and anti-racism. But don't be overwhelmed—we'll take it step by step. We'll first learn the language and concepts of race and racism. Then we can start to think about changes we can make in ourselves, in our communities, and in the world to challenge racism. There are lots of ideas in this book for thinking bigger and learning new skills as we work to stand up to racism all around us.

Imagine a world where everyone is treated fairly and no one is hurt or looked down on because of the color of their skin. Think about all the good that will come when everyone is valued, respected, and cared for— no matter who they are. That's a world worth fighting for, so let's go!

Your friends at American Girl

contents

take anti-racism action 66

stay curious and keep working 100

WHAT IS RACISM?

One little word has a lot packed into it.

starting your journey

If you're reading this book, you're a girl who . . .

is curious.

is brave.

stands up for others.

wants to make the world a better place for everyone.

How do I HELP?

But you might also be a girl who . . .

feels uncomfortable talking about race.

isn't sure what words to use when talking about race.

wants to help fight racism but doesn't know how.

is worried she'll never be able to do enough.

Here's the good news—you can be all these things! You can be brave *and* feel uncomfortable talking about race. You can stand up for others *and* be unsure how to help fight racism. Even grown-ups have these mixed-up feelings. You don't need to be perfect or know everything to begin this work—in fact, no one who is doing this work is flawless. Standing up to racism is a lifelong journey, but it's an exciting one. If you're willing to put yourself out there and learn more about racism, that's enough to get started!

9

what is race?

There are a lot of words and ideas that describe race and racism. It can be overwhelming and confusing. Let's break it down.

Race is a system that's used to sort people into groups based on their ancestry or physical appearance, like skin color. Black, White, Latinx, and Asian are some examples of these categories.

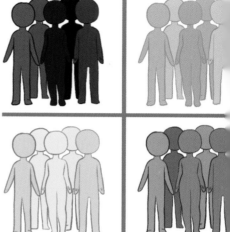

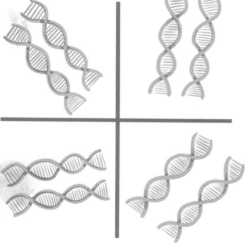

But this is tricky. It's impossible to identify a person's race in her DNA—you won't ever see it under a microscope. There's no gene that determines what group a person belongs to. But we do tend to divide people into groups socially. The idea of biological race isn't real, but society has everyone believing it is.

Those beliefs are so strong that they create stereotypes about whole groups of people. Stereotypes are beliefs or assumptions about groups of people that aren't true. Sometimes we don't even know that we believe a certain stereotype—the idea might have come from a TV show or from something someone said. Even though we aren't aware of it, these thoughts and stereotypes inform how we act. They cause us to prefer certain groups over others through what is called implicit bias—a set of dangerous assumptions that can make us unknowingly hurt others. Our brains automatically make these assumptions about other people. But we can learn to notice our thoughts and then act differently.

But sometimes people treat others badly on purpose. **Bigotry** is treating another person differently because of their race. Bigotry can sound like someone telling a racist "joke," or it can look like not allowing someone to play with you because of her skin color. Anyone can be bigoted because these are personal, individual behaviors.

Racism is how society treats racial groups differently. Racism is so much bigger than bigotry because it is about whole groups of people. In US society, White people have more power in their roles as teachers, school officials, bankers, doctors, or politicians. Because of implicit bias and sometimes on purpose, White people have made it easier for other White people to benefit from systems, such as education, that help them have more successful lives. Whether this happens on purpose or unconsciously, it's still racism.

In this book, you'll see words such as *race* and *racial groups* to describe people. But keep in mind that while these words are common and used everywhere, separating people into groups by race allows some people to feel superior to others, usually based on the color of their skin.

systemic racism

Racism has been around for hundreds of years, and it affects everyone.

Racism creates systems that make sure White people get access to the best education, housing, and jobs. This has been happening over hundreds of years, and it's called **systemic racism.** Did you know that there was a time when people of color could not go to certain schools, live in certain neighborhoods, or have certain jobs? Doing those things was illegal, and they could be punished. These laws prevented them from reaching their full potential and from being able to reach their dreams. Those laws also justified treating someone differently because of their race and made inequality seem normal.

Even though laws have changed, changing people's minds and hearts takes a lot more work. We are still dealing with the impact of stereotypes and racism that started from having these laws. For example, laws kept Black people from living in neighborhoods with White people. White kids went to neighborhood schools that had more resources, like high-quality books and materials. Having gone to schools with more resources, they went on to get better, higher-paying jobs that let them move into even better neighborhoods. The impact of these laws will last for generations, and people of color continue to lose out on good schools, housing, and jobs. That's why it's not enough to just be nice to people of color—we have to practice anti-racism to change the systems that treat them unfairly.

words about race

It can feel really awkward to talk about race and racism. Racial history is unfair and painful, so many people don't like to bring it up. Have you ever started talking about race and a parent shushed you? Have you ever asked a question about race and a teacher skipped to the next subject? Racism remains a big problem for society because people don't talk about it. But we can't make racism better by staying quiet. Here are some words that will help you understand race and racism and how to talk about it.

People of Color: people from racial groups that are not White. Sometimes you might hear the words "underrepresented," "minority," or "marginalized" to describe this group of people.

Black/African American: some prefer to say "African American" to describe Black people because it highlights their shared historical roots in Africa. Others prefer "Black" to emphasize that people with black skin come from different places. In this book, we use "Black" because it's the most inclusive and tends to describe its members most accurately.

Latinx: people who trace their background to Latin American countries. Though "Hispanic" is a common term for this group, it only refers to people from countries that were once under Spanish control, such as Spain, the Philippines, Equatorial Guinea, and some Latin American countries. The word "Latino" more accurately describes people with ties to Latin American countries. But "Latino" technically refers to men, and "Latina" refers to women. "Latinx" refers to all genders.

Native American/ American Indian/ Indigenous: people who trace their ancestry back to the Americas before Europeans came. "Indian" is an inaccurate term from when Christopher Columbus thought he had landed in India. "Native American" acknowledges that people lived here before Europeans came, though some prefer "American Indian." "Indigenous" refers to a nation's earliest known inhabitants.

BIPOC: refers to **B**lack, **I**ndigenous, and **P**eople **o**f **C**olor. Some people use this term to be more inclusive.

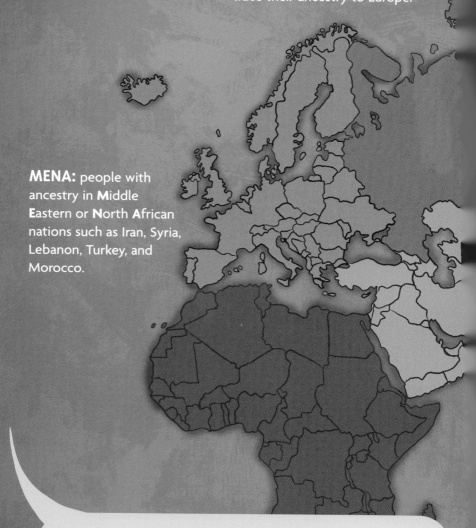

Ally: someone who works together with people of color to make society fairer and more just.

White: people who can usually trace their ancestry to Europe.

MENA: people with ancestry in **M**iddle **E**astern or **N**orth **A**frican nations such as Iran, Syria, Lebanon, Turkey, and Morocco.

How to say it

Sometimes none of these terms are quite right when describing a racial group. It's always best to call people by the name they currently prefer. Those names will continue to change, so research the preferred name for different groups. And if you're talking to someone and don't know the right word, just ask what term they like best.

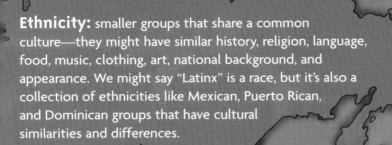

Ethnicity: smaller groups that share a common culture—they might have similar history, religion, language, food, music, clothing, art, national background, and appearance. We might say "Latinx" is a race, but it's also a collection of ethnicities like Mexican, Puerto Rican, and Dominican groups that have cultural similarities and differences.

Asian American: people living in the United States who can trace their ancestry back to an Asian country. Ethnicities within this group include Chinese Americans, Korean Americans, Japanese Americans, Filipino Americans, and Indian Americans.

Multiracial: people who identify with or belong to more than one racial group. Multiracial people have always existed, and the number of children with mixed-race parents is growing.

Pacific Islander: people who can trace their ancestry to a region of the South Pacific Ocean called Oceania.

17

same day, different experiences

Selah and Madison are sixth-graders at the same middle school. But their days look very different.

MADISON

Madison wears her hair in a ponytail, like most of her friends, and they rarely comment on it.

Most of the books in the library are about people who look like Madison.

Madison's history class focuses on White people and their experiences.

Madison is never the only White person in any of her classes.

SELAH

People often want to touch Selah's hair to see how it feels.

It's hard for Selah to find books in the library about girls who look like her.

Selah often stands out as the only Black girl in her classes.

The fact is, Madison's life is often easier in ways she doesn't even notice. That's because the world she lives in was built to favor White people. Selah, on the other hand, runs into obstacles every day that make her feel different, discouraged, and even invisible.

In Selah's classes, the people and experiences she learns about almost never look like her.

19

becoming anti-racist

It's not fair that just because Madison is White, her life is easier. But Madison is not mean to Selah and never calls her inappropriate names. She's not racist! But is that enough? To make things more equal for Selah and help stop racism for everyone, Madison can learn to be anti-racist.

Anti-racism is when people work to make society more fair and help people of color get the same quality of education, housing, jobs, food, and safety that most White people have. Everyone can practice anti-racism.

Many people try not to be racist and think it's enough to avoid using racist terms or to not tell racist jokes. Some act like differences don't exist and strive to treat everyone the same.

These actions help people feel that they are doing enough to combat racism, but they don't really help people of color get the same kind of education or jobs that many White people have. That's why it's important to be anti-racist—all of us have to purposely work to create real and meaningful changes for *everyone*.

Why is race such a big deal?

Think about society as an after-school club. Lucy, who is White, is the president of the Drama Club. She is in charge of handing out cookies to other kids. She might give the cookies only to tall kids or only to kids whose last names start with D. It's completely unfair, but, hey, Lucy's in charge!

As the United States was forming, the leaders among the European newcomers took land from Native Americans, waged war against people who'd be called Mexicans, and enslaved Black people. Why? One reason is they believed in granting more favorable treatment according to skin color. The idea of race has stuck around so long because the people in power (like Lucy) have decided who gets "cookies."

Cookies for **TALL** People **ONLY!**

Selah doesn't get one because she's a scatterbrain.

Now, imagine Lucy gives Madison a cookie but doesn't give one to Selah. To make everyone think that she is being fair, Lucy might accuse Selah of being too scatterbrained to deserve a cookie. Armed with this excuse, Lucy hands out cookies unfairly, and everyone starts thinking it's right, natural, and even a good thing that Selah doesn't get any cookies. The rest of the Drama Club accepts Lucy's excuses as the truth.

21

history of racism

Racism works the same way as Lucy handing out the cookies. Throughout history, many scientists said some racial groups were inferior and should not be treated the same way as other "superior" racial groups. Some psychologists said certain races weren't capable enough to appreciate rights such as owning land or voting. Some educators claimed people of color weren't smart enough to deserve equality in learning. Some religious leaders even said certain racial groups weren't worthy of free-dom. Powerful people in science, psychology, education, religion, law, politics, and media said over and over that race and racial differences were real. Others began to adopt those beliefs, and the false idea of race was turned into an excuse to not share the "cookies" fairly.

White supremacy

The idea that the White race is superior to all other races is called **White supremacy.** For a long time, White people in power claimed that science proved they were superior and used that false claim as the excuse to take over land, enslave people, and even murder non-White people. Now, White supremacy also means that there's a system in place where White people control society, make the rules for others, and make sure that White people benefit the most from that power.

Why does racism persist?

Imagine that Lucy makes a rule that the Drama Club should never give cookies to Selah or people who look like her. Ever. After a while, the other club members start believing that it's natural, good, and right that Selah doesn't get cookies. Even Madison, who is nice and friendly, might start to think this is the way things should be.

Centuries of laws, rules, and social codes have trained people to think racial inequality is normal. At first, the unfairness of the Lucys was obvious, but after years and years, the inequalities became "just the way things are" and nice people like Madison went along with them. Racism starts with individuals, but it survives when it becomes the shared beliefs of an entire society.

white privilege

When people talk about **White privilege,** they mean that White people get certain advantages whether or not they want them, and those advantages often lead to greater power in almost every aspect of life. White people get these things just because of the color of their skin. Even if Madison treats Selah with kindness, or even if Madison dedicates herself to practicing anti-racism, she will always get cookies and have privileges and benefits just because of her skin color. White privilege can feel invisible to White people. But for people of color, it often means feeling unaccepted or unwanted.

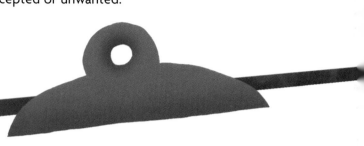

white privilege checklist

Check all the situations that apply to you.

- ☐ I can browse in a store without an employee following me, as if I'm about to steal something.
- ☐ I see models and actors who look like me on billboards and in videos, movies, and magazines.
- ☐ People assume I can speak English.
- ☐ Most of the historical stories that I have been told are about people who look like me.
- ☐ When I get an award or recognition, no one says it's because of my skin color.
- ☐ I can find hair products that work on my hair type, and the food that my family eats is in the regular areas of the store, not in a separate "ethnic" area.
- ☐ It's easy to find books in my library about girls like me or with pictures that look like me.
- ☐ When I need a bandage, I can easily find one that matches my skin tone.

USE your PRIVILEGE for GOOD

If you checked any of these statements, you might have White privilege. If you have White privilege, that's OK. But what you do with that privilege matters. Use it to make the world good for all people!

When Lucy gives cookies to the White girls in the Drama Club, Madison might think it's wrong. She could throw her cookie on the ground and say so, but the rules still guarantee her right to a cookie. If Madison really wants to do something to fight her privilege, she could give half of her cookie to Selah. Then the girls could work together to change the rules.

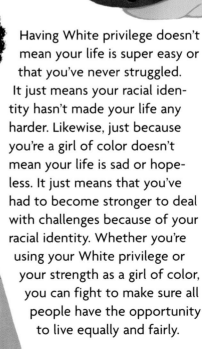

Having White privilege doesn't mean your life is super easy or that you've never struggled. It just means your racial identity hasn't made your life any harder. Likewise, just because you're a girl of color doesn't mean your life is sad or hopeless. It just means that you've had to become stronger to deal with challenges because of your racial identity. Whether you're using your White privilege or your strength as a girl of color, you can fight to make sure all people have the opportunity to live equally and fairly.

identity

All of us have words we use or ways to describe ourselves.

Sometimes we might identify ourselves by our family members.

Or we might group ourselves by age or grade.

A lot of times, we describe ourselves or others by race or skin tone.

There are so many ways to identify ourselves. When all the layers of who we are come together, it's called **intersectionality.** That's the idea that we are not just one fixed thing—our identities are complex. Intersectionality lets you celebrate all the qualities that make you special. But it's also a way to see how easy or difficult it is for you to move through the world.

Privilege and intersectionality go hand in hand. Think about some words that describe you and write them down. It might look something like this:

Some of those identities might give you an advantage in the world. If you are White, you probably receive better treatment just because of your skin color. At the same time, some parts of your identity might be a disadvantage. Sometimes being a girl means you're discriminated against—just for being a girl. Or if you're the lowest grade in your school, you might get fewer freedoms than an older kid.

The thing is, your experience will be very different from someone who seems just like you. It's important to look at a person's complete identity. No matter what, who you are is always going to be someone to celebrate. And we all deserve to be treated with respect, kindness, and fairness.

unzipping the truth about racism

There are a lot of opinions and ideas about stereotypes, biases, and racism. But some ideas people have just aren't true. Read each statement below and decide whether it's true or false.

1. If I try hard enough, I can escape having any biases. It's possible for me to see everything—and everyone—without judgment.

    True   **False**

2. Having White privilege means my life has been easy.

    True   **False**

3. Talking about racial issues divides people and is anti-American.

    True   **False**

4. I don't see someone's race. I only see the person.

    True   **False**

5. Racism no longer exists and hasn't been around for a long time.

    True   **False**

6. People of color actually have it easier than White people.

    True   **False**

7. Anyone can be racist, even people of color.

    True   **False**

8. People are too sensitive. If I don't mean what I say or do to be racist, it won't be.

    True   **False**

Answers

1. False. Everyone has biases, and sometimes we don't even know where they came from—they are just a part of who we are. You can work to get rid of them, and until that happens, do your best to manage them.

2. False. Having White privilege means racism hasn't made your life more difficult. Accepting that you've had racial privilege doesn't mean ignoring other hardships. It just means that your race hasn't created barriers to success.

3. False. Racism has divided the United States and undermines the nation's values of equality and liberty. The goal of talking about problems is to fix them, which is a unifying and pro-American ideal.

4. False. Everyone makes racial assumptions. Don't try to ignore racial differences—you'll never be able to! When you ignore someone's race, you're ignoring an important part of who they are. Celebrate differences and treat people justly regardless of race.

5. False. Public acceptance of blatant discrimination might have declined, but some aspects of racial inequality (such as income and wealth) are worse today than they were in 1940. We still have a lot of work to do to make our world anti-racist.

6. False. Some claim racism harms White people because of policies intended to help minority groups attend college and enter the workforce. Those programs were designed to fix racism, and over time, most of them have disappeared. Still, some people point to these efforts to claim people of color have it better than Whites, even though the problem of racial inequalities has not been fixed.

7. False. Anyone can be bigoted and believe that a racial group is superior to others. They can say or do mean things to others based on race. But systemic racism is social inequality in food, housing, employment, income, education, law enforcement, imprisonment, legal protection, political representation, and cultural representation. It is these systems, not individual bigots, that create racial inequality.

8. False. Racism is not based on intent. It's based on how another person feels it. This makes racism and bigotry complicated, but no one has the right to tell other people how to feel about their experiences.

RACISM

AND YOU

Becoming anti-racist starts by looking inward.

getting started

By practicing anti-racism, you work to make lives better for people of color. But that's a big challenge! The idea of improving schools for Mexican Americans or getting better jobs for Native Americans feels overwhelming and impossible to accomplish. You might think, "I'm just one person. How can I help?" Start small by noticing what you *can* do.

NEIGHBORS

School

friends

family

BOOK CLUB

My mini-worlds

Imagine your world as a collection of bubbles—these are the miniature societies you're a part of. Your family is your closest bubble. Other bubbles include your friends, your neighbors, your school, and other groups you belong to. Even if you feel as though you don't have power to create big change in the world, there are smaller bubbles where you do have influence.

Once you've identified who is in your bubbles, you can pinpoint ways to share your opinions and knowledge with others. A dinner conversation can help your younger brother understand anti-racism. Or asking your book club to read a book by a Black author whose main character is different from the main characters in other books you've read can encourage your friends to see more perspectives. The idea is to expand the thinking within your mini-worlds to include new and different points of view.

living inside a bubble

Thinking about our bubbles is helpful because they show who's closest to us, but they can also cause problems. We often don't see what life is like outside our bubbles. For example, because she's a member of the Drama Club with a cookie, Madison might have a hard time knowing what it's like for Selah to not have one. And neither Madison nor Selah may fully grasp why some people get a cookie and others don't until they identify the pattern.

What shapes your world?

Most White people live in mostly White neighborhoods, go to mostly White schools, and hang out with other White people. They generally read books and watch movies and TV shows about White people. It becomes easy for White people to assume everyone lives like them—or *should* live like them. Why? Because they are living inside their bubble. But think about what it's like for people who live outside that bubble.

What's going on outside?

How might it feel if you . . .

- didn't have books, shows, or movies with characters who looked like you?

- didn't have school lessons about people who looked like you?

  - went to a school with a dress code that didn't allow you to wear your hair the way it grows out of your head?

  - were the only member of your racial group in most places?

- learned more than one language and then people made fun of you for having an accent?

ARRING

NO ONE WHO LOOKS LIKE YOU!

coming this NOVEMBER

HISTORY

The Declaration of Dependence

YOUR HAIRSTYLE

SCHOOL RULES

The problem with bubbles

When we are inside our bubbles, we feel safe and comfortable, and we start to believe our way of living is the right way—or the only way. Inside your bubble, you might forget that not everyone lives like you. Those outside your bubble may dress differently, act differently, or talk differently, but that doesn't mean that their lives are bad, wrong, or less worthy. And too often, those on the outside are made to feel more stupid, ugly, and bad than those inside. If you stay inside your bubble and don't recognize that differences are good, you're going to miss out on a lot of great experiences!

MY BUBBLE

outside your bubble

People who aren't in your bubble probably live a different life than you do. For example, Madison and Lucy might assume that Selah's life is the same as theirs because they all go to the same school, enjoy Drama Club, have similar family structures, and share the same hopes and worries about their future. But Lucy and Madison don't realize how different life is for Selah. She has other issues, such as people constantly wanting to touch her hair or never getting lead roles in Drama Club productions because people believe that some roles can only be played by White people.

Living in your bubble makes it feel like your way of doing things is the only way to do things. If you have access to good food, clothing, jobs, education, housing, and safety, it might be hard to realize how hard life is for people who don't. Worst of all, your bubble will give you all kinds of reasons to think others shouldn't have these things.

Think about your bubble and answer these questions:

What is life like for others or people who are different from me?

How do I feel about those people?

What am I missing out on by only living inside my bubble?

Maybe you've never had to think about people outside your bubble before, so you might have trouble answering these questions. Read on to learn some skills for getting outside your bubble.

beyond your bubble

To venture outside your bubble, start by thinking about what you want to learn. Ask yourself, What do I want to know? How do I want to grow?

If you were trying to learn something new in history class, what would you do? You'd probably think about where you could get that information—whether by reading, researching, or talking to other people. To learn about the experiences of others, you can do the same thing. Make a learning plan by pinpointing what you want to learn, how you're going to learn it, and how you'll share what you've learned with others.

Mini-challenges

How many of these can you do to expand your bubble?

- [ ] With a parent or teacher, find five videos that help you learn about others' life experiences and points of view.

- [ ] Ask a librarian to help you look up articles about anti-racism or discover three books by authors of color whose main characters live in bubbles unlike yours.

- [ ] Learn another language, even if it's just some basic vocabulary or a few phrases.

- [ ] Watch a show or movie featuring people from a different racial group.

- [ ] Listen to a different kind of music than you usually do.

- [ ] Research your community to learn about the racial minorities in your city. Are there cultural events put on by those groups you could attend?

- [ ] Find recipes to make food you've never tried before. Or seek out a new restaurant for your family's next night out!

- [ ] Spin a globe and place your finger on a random spot. Research that country's people, food, music, art, history, politics, and culture.

Be Anti-RACIST

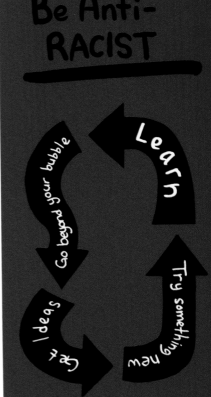

Go beyond your bubble

Learn

Try something new

Get Ideas

Going beyond your bubble can be fun! But be careful: If you're a White girl, spending an afternoon watching a movie about a Black girl doesn't mean you understand her life, her story, or the experiences of other Black people. Anti-racism is a lifelong process! Madison can try to understand what life is like for Selah, but she will never fully get it. It's still important to keep trying to better understand other people and their experiences.

looking through your lens

If you wear glasses, you know that you see things differently when you take your glasses off. In the same way, your bubble can be like a lens that influences how you see the world.

Seeing what's real

Some lenses make White people look good, hardworking, trustworthy, and kind but make people of color look bad, lazy, mean, and dangerous. Even people who want to fight racism have bigoted thoughts and see people of color with fear, suspicion, or distrust. Why? One reason is because the lens we use to look at people outside our bubbles causes us to see stereotypes of people instead of who they really are.

How you **See** people CAN HELP **IMPROVE** ≡ THEIR ≡ future

Sometimes stereotypes lump all people from the same race together and create assumptions about an entire group of people. An example of a stereotype is that *all* Black people are great athletes or that *all* Asian Americans are math whizzes. It might be true that some people in a group align with a stereotype, but no stereotype is true for all the people in a group. Big statements like that aren't true about *any* group! But when we never encounter people outside our own bubbles, we might believe those false stereotypes.

What are some stereotypes that you are aware of? What are some stereotypes about the group *you* belong to?

Has anyone made assumptions about you based on your age? At some point in your life, you've probably had to explain to an adult that you are capable of doing something basic—like making your own breakfast—when they assumed you couldn't handle that task. Looking at you through that lens—that is, a stereotype based on your age—an adult made an assumption about you that isn't true. How does it make you feel when someone assumes just because you're a kid, you can't handle independence and responsibility?

This is how people of color can feel much of the time. Imagine how Selah feels in a club, school, and society where people assume negative things about her just because of the color of her skin.

implicit bias

Your bubble creates the lens through which you see the world.
Things like where you grew up, who your family is, the color of
your skin, the videos you watch, the books you read, and the
education you receive influence how you view others. No matter how hard you try to see everyone the same, your lens makes
you like certain kinds of people more than others. A lot of TV
programs and movies unfairly show more men of color committing
violent crimes, and if you see that image over and over again,
you'll be more likely to fear men of color. This is called **implicit
bias** (sometimes it's called **unconscious bias**).

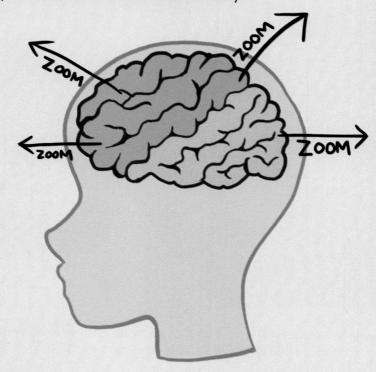

As your brain creates shortcuts for understanding the world, it will
assume that all people in groups who are shown as dangerous on TV or
in movies are also dangerous in everyday life, even though they aren't.
Instead of seeing individuals, your brain sees them as members of a
group. And your mind will associate certain groups with certain types of
behaviors. And before you know it, you're thinking or acting in a bigoted
way. Everyone has these implicit biases, and most people aren't even
aware that the biases affect their thoughts and actions.

Some common implicit biases

- Hearing someone speaking another language and assuming they can't also speak English.

- Seeing a girl wearing a headscarf and assuming she was not born in the United States.

- Going into a neighborhood with lots of families of color and assuming it's not safe.

Hi! I am Maha from Wisconsin.

How do you stop implicit bias? You can't stop it completely, but you can manage it. Slow down. Don't rush to judgment. Ask yourself questions that force you to connect your assumptions to specific behaviors. Do you assume a classmate from a particular group is lazy, stupid, or scary? Is your brain relying on shortcuts rather than that person's actual behaviors? Ask yourself these kinds of questions to slow down your implicit biases.

are you ready for new lenses?

Check the statements that might be true about you.

★ I like that Wednesday mornings are "Waffle Wednesdays" no matter what!

♥ I love to rearrange the furniture in my room—it always feels like a brand-new space even with the same stuff.

★ My friends know that when they come over for my birthday, they'll always get double chocolate cupcakes with lots of rainbow sprinkles!

♥ When I get my hair cut, you can count on me trying something new. I love a fresh look!

★ I've read my favorite book so many times I can't count. It always makes me feel good.

♥ When my dad surprises us with one of his new recipes, I'm excited. He's a great cook!

★ Going to the same camp every summer is my favorite week of the year.

♥ If there's an after-school club I want to join, I'll try it even if my friends aren't interested. Why not?

★ I've played goalie on my soccer team since I can remember.

♥ I think it would be so fun if my family went on a vacation, but our parents didn't tell us where we were going first.

If you chose mostly stars, you know what you like! Consider exploring new experiences or ideas, even if it means not eating waffles on Wednesdays. When you start to mix it up, you'll discover new foods, books, and activities that will light up your life. Go for it—you have nothing to lose!

If you chose mostly hearts, you're ready for a new challenge—and a new way to view the world! You'll never say no to a different way of thinking or a new experience. Use your enthusiasm to get others excited about learning and trying out different foods, cultural celebrations, books, and movies.

Flip the script

How you think and talk about differences is a big deal. Just because something isn't what you like or grew up doing doesn't mean it's wrong or bad. By being curious and learning more, you can change your thinking to celebrate differences.

When you encounter something new, how do you react? Do you turn your nose up at new foods or stare at people who are wearing clothing that's different from yours? Use these ideas to change your mindset.

Instead of saying (or thinking):

That head covering looks dumb.

Ew! What's in your lunch?

Your parents don't speak English?!

I would never eat that.

That sounds like a weird way to celebrate a holiday.

Flip the script! Try:

Your headscarf is so pretty. Can you tell me what it's called so I use the right word?

I've never seen rice like that. What's in it?

That's cool you know another language!

Can I try some? I've never tasted that.

How fun! I've never thought of that.

For all of these—different foods, ways of dressing, and traditions—you can follow up with, "Can you tell me more?"

question your biases

Living in a society full of powerful, bigoted stereotypes, it can feel impossible to think that we have the ability to change the way we view people. But working to question our implicit biases helps us see more clearly. Here's how:

Slow down and ask questions. Instead of making quick (and probably wrong) assumptions about someone, ask yourself: What assumptions do I have about this person? Why do I think that?

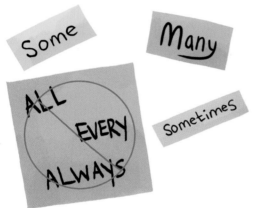

Be accurate. Replace broad language like "all," "every," and "always" with more accurate words like "some," "many," and "sometimes." Remember that thing about stereotypes? When we say *all* people in a group are a certain way, we're making harmful assumptions.

Be specific. Instead of thinking to yourself at the store, "That guy is acting weird," you might think, "That person is taking a really long time picking out spaghetti sauce." When you're specific, many actions don't seem that unusual or scary.

Examine yourself. Ask yourself why you have the beliefs you do about others and where those beliefs come from. Is there a way to think more inclusively about people?

Widen your experience. Fill your mind with positive images of other groups by watching diverse shows and reading books about all kinds of people. Those images will counter the stereotypes you encounter, and it'll help you see people how they really are.

Practice. And then practice some more. Everyone's lenses get smudged from time to time, but by continuing to work on anti-racism goals, we'll all see more clearly.

Madison might think that it's Selah's fault or make other assumptions about why she didn't get a cookie. But if Madison slows down, she might realize all the bad things she thinks about Selah actually come from bad things Lucy has said about Selah—or people like her. Madison might also believe popular racial stereotypes, and that could cloud the way she sees Selah. Even Selah might believe some of these assumptions. That's how powerful racial stereotypes can be. When Madison and Selah clean up their lenses, they see what's really true.

47

tough times ahead

As you begin practicing anti-racist thinking and actions, you might run into a few hurdles. Here are some tips.

WHAT IF?

I live in a place where everybody looks the same.

TRY

It might be hard to learn about different ethnicities when everyone in your life lives inside your bubble and looks the same. Use books, articles, TV shows, documentaries, and movies to learn about others' experiences. Go back to the mini-challenges on page 39 and check more items off the list. You're not limited by where you live—there's so much out there to discover!

feel awkward widening
my perspective.

TRY

We feel comfortable in our bubbles, so it will feel strange going beyond them. A great way to start is to follow your curiosity. Try attending cultural events—like a public Diwali event in your city—and ask questions about what's going on. If you're at a potluck and someone brings a Hmong dish to share, ask for more details. Finding moments to learn about the foods, sights, and sounds around us can create opportunities for more personal conversations about names, hobbies, schools, and friends.

Think about how you've made friends in other new situations, like at camp or with a new team. You were probably friendly and curious. You asked questions to get to know another person and shared info about your life, too. Use those same skills to get over the awkwardness of meeting new people who just happen to be from outside your bubble.

WHAT IF?

I'm researching, but I'm not finding enough information. I feel stuck.

TRY

Go to your school or public library, and ask the librarian to help you find the kinds of books or movies you're interested in. With a parent's permission, you can search online, but stick to websites that end in .gov, .edu, or .org, because those sites will probably have the most accurate information.

WHAT IF?

I'm overwhelmed! It seems too BIG for me.

TRY

A lot of the things you'll learn might make you sad and angry. The first step to practicing anti-racism is recognizing racism and the harm it has had on our society. When you look beyond your bubble, you might learn some tough truths or feel guilty. This work is hard, so be sure to reach out for support when you need it—you don't have to do this all by yourself. You're creating positive change in the world because you care. That's something to feel good about!

changing behaviors

Once you venture beyond the bubbles that separate you from others and keep you from seeing them clearly, it's time to examine the thoughts, words, and actions that help make society fairer and those that don't.

Before you can change your behaviors, you have to start with these four steps:

1. Acknowledge your biases. Madison needs to recognize her bigoted thoughts about Selah and realize that they're hurtful.

2. Challenge your thoughts. Madison needs to change her thinking by challenging the assumptions she has about Selah.

Selah can't audition for a lead in the next Drama Club performance because Black girls can never be leads . . . right?

Actually, why do I think that? It's probably because we have never had a Black girl play a lead character. Also, Lucy's always telling me that Selah isn't talented, but that's definitely not true.

3. Take action. Figure out what you are going to do to support your anti-racist thinking.

Selah is talented and she should be able to try out for any character, just like all the White girls do. I'm going to personally invite her to audition with me. And I'm going to talk to the other Drama Club members about allowing and encouraging anyone from any race to play any type of role.

4. Practice, practice, practice. To replace bad habits with good ones, you've got to practice. The same goes for bigoted thoughts and actions. This isn't easy work. You'll find yourself thinking the same old thoughts you've always had. You'll find yourself in new situations and need to start at step 1 again and again. But now you know better and you can challenge yourself to strengthen your anti-racist beliefs.

blatant discrimination

Some people don't want to go outside their bubble, and they might think of everyone else as outsiders and not value their experiences. This can lead to **blatant discrimination.** *Blatant* means doing something openly and unashamedly. This type of bigotry is usually easy to see.

Blatant discrimination can involve bigoted ideas about people's skin color, hair texture, or eye shape. It can be making fun of the food, music, dress, language, art, and religious practices of different groups. Often, blatant discrimination stems from stereotypes about people being lazy, stupid, disgusting, or dangerous. Often, people do this to remind others they don't belong inside the bubble.

These are all examples of blatant discrimination. These words and behaviors are right out in the open and everyone can see them.

But I was just joking!

When people do these mean things, they might say, "I'm just joking" if someone questions them. They might accuse their critics of being overly sensitive or not having a sense of humor. They could say their comments are being blown out of proportion or that people are trying to make the situation about race when it's not. These are common reactions among people who are called out for committing acts of bigotry.

If Lucy makes a joke about why she won't ever give Selah a cookie, Madison could say, "Hey, that's not cool. Selah deserves a cookie, too." Selah could even say, "What you said isn't funny, and it hurt my feelings." Lucy probably won't like being called out, and she might respond, "Whoa, lighten up! I was just joking!" No matter what, Selah receives the message loud and clear: "You're not welcome!"

Being anti-racist is not about teaching Selah to learn how to take a joke or trying to understand what Lucy really means to say. To be true anti-racists, Madison and Selah should help Lucy realize how her words impact Selah. The point isn't to preserve the Drama Club's bubble. The point is to make it more welcoming to people like Selah.

microaggressions

Blatant discrimination is the big and obvious things people do to keep people out of their bubble, but **microaggressions** are the countless little things people do to exclude others. Sometimes people aren't even aware that they are acting this way. Microaggressions can be as harmful as blatant discrimination, but because they are difficult to recognize, they're hard to call out.

Is this a microaggression?

Read the following scenarios and decide whether a microaggression is taking place.

1. Georgia is welcoming new girl Zoya to her middle school. As they walk around the school library, Georgia asks Zoya, "But where are you really from?"

Yes   No

2. Lauren is swinging her little brother at the playground. A little girl and her mom come up to the swings, and the mom says to Lauren's brother, "Oh, you are so cute! Biracial kids are sooooooo beautiful!"

Yes   No

3. Harper and her teammates are getting ready for soccer practice. Harper goes over to Sophie, pats her hair, and exclaims, "Super fluffy!"

Yes   No

4. Ayla just joined the after-school rocket club, and Fiona asks her what other clubs she's in. When Ayla says she's also in the running club, Fiona responds, "Wow, you don't sound Black at all!"

Yes   No

5. Viviana and Emory are shopping for a birthday present for Emory's younger brother. Whenever they go into a store, a clerk follows Emory around.

Yes   No

6. Priti and Grace are walking into an all-school spelling bee. Grace groans and says, "I'm so bad at spelling! You're probably going to win. You guys always do."

Yes   No

7. Sam is eating a peanut butter and jelly sandwich for lunch, and her friend Sejal is eating chicken biryani. Sejal says, "Huh. You call that a lunch?"

Yes   No

Answers

1. Yes. By asking where Zoya is "really from," Georgia is implying that Zoya doesn't belong here because she looks different from other people Georgia knows.

2. Yes. When the mom says that biracial kids are are "sooooooo beautiful," she's making a value statement based on skin color. Lauren hears that her dark skin isn't beautiful or worthy of praise.

3. Yes. It's wrong to touch someone else without permission, including their hair. Sophie is more than her hair, and just because Sophie and Harper have different types of hair doesn't mean that Sophie's hair is a novelty to be petted and praised.

4. Yes. Fiona may have been trying to be kind with her comment to Ayla, but what's she's really saying is that Ayla is doing a good job fitting into Fiona's bubble and what Fiona thinks is worthy: talking like she does.

5. Yes. Often, people of color are followed in stores because shop owners assume they will steal something just because of their skin color.

6. Yes. Grace is believing the stereotype that all Indians are good at spelling. It makes Priti feel bad that Grace is judging her by her ethnicity, not by who she is.

7. No. Though it's not a very nice thing to say, Sejal's comment isn't based on a racial stereotype. It might hurt Sam's feelings, but it won't make her feel different or bad just because she's White.

On their own, each microaggression may seem small and meaningless, but all these little actions add up, making everyday encounters difficult or hurtful.

Microaggressions lead to discrimination

Let's say that as Lucy passed out the cookies in Drama Club, she said to Selah, "These cookies are only for girls who will be stars someday." Even a little jab like that can intimidate Selah and discourage her from trying out for lead roles. Years later, when it comes time to apply to theater programs at colleges, Selah can't get a letter of recommendation from her drama teacher because she never performed in a lead role. Because Lucy, Madison, and the other girls did have leads, they are able to get into universities that take their acting careers to the next level, while Selah's never even gets off the ground. Why? Because a little microaggression kept her out of the bubble.

It can be lonely to be from an underrepresented group who faces discrimination in small or big ways day after day. Think about how you feel when you have a class without anyone from your friend group. Now imagine what it's like to be the only one from your ethnicity in a situation. For many people of color, this is a common experience. Many people of color spend their entire education and career being the only person from their group among all White people. It's not necessary to experience blatant discrimination to feel excluded.

being an ally

An **ally** is someone who is on your side. Anti-racist allies have to do more than not be mean, not use bigoted words, not believe stereotypes, not call people names, or not make fun of others. Allies go further—they are intentional in their thoughts, words, and actions to help create positive change for people of color.

Intent and impact

"Well, aren't you cute!" Has an adult ever called you "cute," "special," or "adorable" in a way that made you feel like a baby? The person might be trying to be nice, but if they think your clothes, hair, or way of talking is "simply delightful," it can feel insulting. After all, you are much more complex and interesting than that! The person who called you cute was probably well-intentioned, but the impact you felt was negative and made you feel small.

Identity is personal. A person's background is important to who they are. While expressing interest, try not to reduce them to someone who is just "fun," "interesting," or "cool." Sometimes racial identity can come from a history of pain or struggle. Remember to be compassionate and sensitive when talking with others about their backgrounds.

It's good to be curious and ask questions as you get to know someone. But drilling someone about her racial identity can feel invasive. A person's background can be very private and personal, so if you start asking a lot of questions, it can make a person feel uncomfortable. If you're White and attend a mostly White school and start talking about race with one of the few students of color, it might feel like you are shining a light on her differences, not just being curious.

The point of being an anti-racist ally is to help others. If you do or say something that ends up hurting others, even when you meant to be helpful, own up to it, apologize, and ask how you can help. Even as you look outside your bubble, parts of who you are might stay inside. You might be accused of being biased, naive, stupid, privileged, or even racist by the people you're trying to help. If you're honest with yourself, you might recognize those accusations to be true. Think about how your thoughts and actions might unintentionally support the same racial injustice you're trying to fight. And keep trying to do better.

celebrating differences

If someone acts, dresses, or talks differently than you, that doesn't mean they are weird, gross, or wrong. It simply means they are different. Different is good. Imagine if we were all the same—life would be so *boring*!

Pay attention to situations when you judge others who are different. Notice when you start thinking something is weird, gross, dangerous, stupid, wrong, lazy, or sloppy. It can seem that way because of your bubble and the lenses you look through. You might think Indian food is gross, but to more than a billion Indian people in the world, that food is delicious! Your bubble and your lenses create big differences between how you see the world and how the world actually is. Slow down and think about things from different perspectives. New doesn't mean wrong. It just means new. Open yourself up to the history, culture, and traditions of people outside your bubble.

"I don't see color"

Appreciating differences is a huge step in becoming anti-racist. Recognizing that differences are good is a key part of being an ally. You might hear a well-intentioned person say, "I don't see color—I just see a person." But that person isn't celebrating differences; they might be trying to make everyone fit in their bubble. It's important to see—and acknowledge—our differences.

Ignoring all the wonderful ways each of us is different is never going to fight racism. We must see and celebrate what makes us unique—acknowledging our differences is what helps us learn, be more open, and be less judgmental. The point is to accept all our differences, and that those differences should not mean some get treated better or have more opportunities than others.

TAKE

ANTI-RACISM

ACTION

Now you're ready to take anti-racism action. Here's how.

feeling uncomfortable

We've spent a lot of time thinking about what's going on inside ourselves and how we can change our thinking to be anti-racist. But it's not enough to just improve your thinking. You've got to help others. To fight racism, you have to take action and work to improve society. This can be scary. But it's time to start using your voice to make change, even if it makes you uncomfortable. This is often where allies get stuck—they believe in anti-racism work, but it takes a lot of effort and can feel awkward.

This section gives you lots of ways to begin your anti-racism work. You don't have to do everything at once! Take small steps in meeting new friends who share your passion and in taking on projects that create meaningful change. Stay focused, and go at the speed that's right for you. There are so many things you can do to create an environment of anti-racism where everyone can thrive.

start small

A great—and fun!—way to start taking action is to make a new friend. It can be intimidating to take that first step toward a new friendship, especially if the person lives in a different bubble. But just because you're making new kinds of friends, the techniques are the same.

Ten tips for making new friends outside your bubble

1. Introduce yourself. Smile and say hi. (Yes, it's that easy.)

2. Ask questions, but don't grill. Start slow and basic without getting too personal.

3. Don't rush things. Bonds take time to form.

4. Offer invitations. Think of activities around shared interests you can do together.

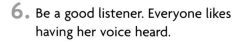

5. Find things to laugh about together— tell jokes or make funny videos.

6. Be a good listener. Everyone likes having her voice heard.

7. If you mess up, say you're sorry.

8. Be real. True friendship is built on being exactly who you are.

9. Make a strong personal connection before talking about sensitive topics like race.

10. If a friendship doesn't form, that's OK. Not everyone is going to click!

Discussing music or celebrities might seem silly, but it can start friendships. And practicing anti-racism means making friends and building trust with people from racial groups other than your own.

Things to talk about

Books Sports Teachers School Collections Free time Hobbies Weekend plans Holidays Music Favorite colors Shows Birthdays Pets Video games Families Favorite foods Movies

Things to do

Paint with watercolors Bake a cake Dance Play loud music Write a play Read the same book Host a party Ride bikes Practice soccer drills Join a club together Volunteer Play hopscotch Eat ice cream Shoot hoops Go for a walk swing Watch a movie Make crafts Have a sleepover

To the rescue?

As you make new friends outside your bubble and become an anti-racism ally, be careful not to assume others need saving or that you're the rescuer. Has someone ever tried to help you, but it made you feel kind of dumb and helpless? Someone can seem like she's having a hard time and actually be fine. Someone can look like she's lonely when she really just likes being alone. To check if someone needs help, you can offer. Just say, "Hey, if you ever need any help, I'm here."

when bigots are also bullies

While it's good to assume that people don't need you to save them, there are times when it's appropriate to step in. Name-calling, making fun of a kid's ethnic background, mocking someone's accent, and bringing up stereotypes are all forms of bigoted bullying. In most situations, bullies target people who are already lonely, scared, and outnumbered. In a school with mostly White kids, students of color might already feel like they don't belong. When a White classmate makes fun of a person of color for the way she looks, talks, dresses, eats, or acts, it makes the person feel even worse. How do you stand up to these bullies?

DO
Focus on the target, not the bully
Sometimes people are so focused on standing up to the bully that they forget about the target. Don't put so much effort on fighting racism that you forget to stand up for those being hurt. For example, ask the target if she is OK.

DO
Change the topic
Redirecting everyone's attention will break the tension of the situation. Talk about anything—the weather, your new puppy, or the upcoming school play. Just keep the conversation moving.

DO
Disrupt the moment
Take the bully aside or ask the target to come with you as you walk away. The idea is to split up the bully, the target, and anyone watching. If it's happening online, you might invite the target to leave that digital space together.

DO
Ask questions

When the situation has cooled, and you feel safe, you can ask the bully questions to encourage deeper thinking about his or her actions. "What happened back there?" or "Why did you say that?" are good starters. Your role as an ally is important here—you're asking the bully to examine his behavior and hopefully change his perspective.

Focus on actions and their consequences. Avoid starting a sentence with "You."

Focus on the big picture. Move the focus away from one person to how a whole group might feel.

Instead of saying,

> You were a real jerk when you did that,

say,

> When people aren't treated fairly, it's hurtful.

Avoid saying something like,

> You really hurt that girl's feelings,

and instead try,

> When we call Black people names, their feelings get hurt.

DON'T
Attack others
No one will want to venture outside their bubble if they're being attacked or criticized. Try to help people reflect on their words and behaviors without making them shut down.

When to get help

Some bigoted bullying situations might get too big and too unsafe for one girl to handle. Reach out to a parent, teacher, school counselor, or other trusted adult for backup. It's always OK to tell an adult if another person is being picked on because of their race.

Focus on solutions. Instead of fixating on the bad behavior, think about ways the bully can make it right in the future.

Instead of saying,

> You don't listen to others,

you could say,

> The more voices we hear from, the stronger our school will be.

Focus on growth. Not everyone will change their bigoted thinking or behaviors right away. It's important to be patient, kind, and compassionate and allow others to gain awareness at their own pace.

You can say,

> I know this is hard, but it's important to change. I'm here for you.

listen and believe

BE A GOOD LISTENER

When a person of color tells you about her experiences, listen and *believe*. Don't try to soften what happened or try to make her feel like it's not that big of a deal. Don't try to explain what "really happened" or suggest that she didn't understand what happened. You wouldn't want somebody saying that you were overreacting to something hurtful or trying to tell you that you misunderstood your own experience.

It's common to want to dismiss or diminish racism. Hearing stories of injustice can be upsetting. But it's important to listen to understand experiences that differ from your own, even if they make you uncomfortable. Knowing others' stories will help you practice anti-racism.

When you listen to someone talk about her racist experience, don't interrupt. Keep your eyes on her, and don't think about what you're going to say next. Let her talk—and talk and talk, if she needs to. Listening—*really listening*—to a person's stories, needs, and feelings is a great way to be an ally. Offer support by saying things like, "That sounds really hurtful," or "I'm sorry that happened to you."

If you've experienced an injustice because of your race, telling your story can feel scary or overwhelming. The fear of not being believed or listened to might keep you from speaking up. Don't let it! Find a friend you can confide in—someone who will listen and take you seriously. She can stand by you and support you as you share what happened. You're not alone, and you deserve to be heard and believed.

messing up

Lots of people are scared to practice anti-racism because they worry they'll do the wrong thing. They fear that they'll say something that makes people from minority groups feel lonelier and more threatened. Many anti-racists worry that by challenging racism they might end up accidentally supporting it. It's tough, but it's critical to get over that fear.

Being afraid of messing up doesn't help people who experience racism. For example, Madison won't be fully anti-racist if she avoids Selah for fear she'll accidentally make things worse. Madison's anxiety doesn't make Lucy any nicer, get Selah any cookies, or help Selah get a letter of recommendation. Selah might be afraid that things will get worse if she speaks up. And the truth is, they might. But things won't get better if she doesn't. To truly challenge racism, Selah and Madison have to take a risk and share how they truly feel.

Learn From Your Mistakes

Mistakes help you learn

Here's a secret: you're going to make mistakes. And that's OK. Having tough conversations about racism is like learning a new language. You learn some basic vocabulary and a few common phrases, but eventually, you've got to just dive in and start speaking! Trying to have real conversations is the only way you'll learn what you're saying wrong and how to change it. And show yourself some compassion—this is hard work.

When things go wrong

The most important thing to do when you hurt someone is to apologize, right? You probably didn't mean to cause harm, but you did. That's when you have to step up, take a deep breath, and say, "I'm sorry."

Here are some ways to say it:

I'm sorry. I hope you'll give me another chance.

I'm sorry. I didn't mean to offend you. I won't do that again.

I'm sorry I made you feel that way. How can I make it better?

I'm sorry I used that term and upset you. Is there another term I should use?

After apologizing, think about how you can do better next time. And then do that. When you mess up—and everyone does!—say you're sorry, learn from the experience, and move on.

questions from friends

Some of your friends might not be thinking yet about expanding their bubble. When you start standing up against racism, you might have to stand up against a lot of the things that friends in your bubble think are normal. Even if your friends don't practice bigotry on purpose, they might unintentionally say or do racist things.

If you call out a friend for making a bigoted joke, she might think you're acting weird, taking things too seriously, or need to lighten up. For example, if Madison started standing up to Lucy for discriminating against Selah, the rest of the Drama Club might feel like she's also challenging them. Why? Because people inside your bubble might feel threatened or uncomfortable if you question their values.

If this happens, try to understand your friend's point of view, stating your goals, and finding common solutions. If a friend accuses you of being too sensitive, ask, "How should I react instead?" If she says her bigoted actions were just a joke, you could ask, "How do you think those actions impact others?" Listening to your friends is important, but so are your anti-racism goals.

Whatever you say or do, try to explain how you want to make things better for everyone. Show your friends that your goals don't work against them, but are for *everyone*. Focus on how practicing anti-racism can benefit all people, even the ones who criticize you for it.

questions from adults

Trying out your new anti-racist thinking with your parents may make them think you're questioning the values they taught you. They might take your new views as a personal attack on their parenting. This can be scary for parents. They can feel criticized. They grew up in a different time and may need help widening their perspective.

The same is true for teachers or other adults in your life. They might understand your views as criticisms of their values—and no one likes to feel criticized. Ask the adults in your life what they think and why they think it. Starting conversations like this can be challenging, but this is where positive change begins.

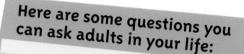

Here are some questions you can ask adults in your life:

- What did you learn about racism in school?
- Did your parents ever talk about race and racism?
- Have you ever witnessed blatant discrimination? What did you do?
- Did you have any friends of a different race when you were in middle school?
- How has racism changed since you were my age?
- Do you know about White privilege? Do you think it applies to you?

Just like with your friends, it helps your parents, teachers, and other adults understand your point of view if you explain your goals. Show that the solutions you are working for are good for everybody. Just because you're trying to help another racial group doesn't mean you're against your own. It means you support all racial groups.

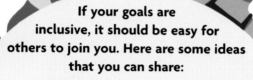

If your goals are inclusive, it should be easy for others to join you. Here are some ideas that you can share:

• I want everyone to feel included.

• I'd like to hear from everyone, not just the kids who usually feel safe speaking up.

• When everyone is treated fairly, we all win!

• People of color have been treated unfairly for too long. I want to change that.

• I like being exposed to a variety of experiences. Opening my mind is good for me.

• I don't think that differences are bad. I want to celebrate all the diversity in my life!

What others would you add? Write your goals on a sticky note and put it on your mirror. Remind yourself every day why you are choosing to be anti-racist.

staying dedicated

To remain dedicated and engaged as an anti-racism activist, learn to have empathy and compassion for others. Empathy is putting yourself in someone else's place and seeing the world from her eyes. Being compassionate means seeing and acting with love, not anger or judgment. Even when we disagree, it's important to treat one another with kindness and patience. If you keep your heart and mind open to diverse experiences and opinions, you're sharpening your empathy and compassion skills and becoming a stronger anti-racism activist.

If your friends or family still don't agree or identify with your need to become more inclusive, you might have to continue practicing anti-racism without their approval. You can still be friends with people who don't support you, and you can still love family members who disagree with you. That's compassion—loving without judgment.

In fact, if you continue to love and support friends and family even when they don't support you in your anti-racism work, your openness might just be what changes their mind. If they see how dedicated you are to helping others and improving the world, they could be inspired to begin doing the same thing.

KINDNESS IS CONTAGIOUS PASS iT AROUND

In the meantime, it's important to be around people who can support you as you practice anti-racism. You need a community of allies to help you learn and take anti-racism actions.

practicing compassion

It takes work to be compassionate. Here are some tips for practicing compassion with others:

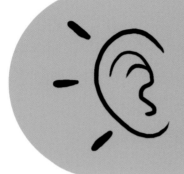

Listen to understand, not to defend your own opinion. When you are fully listening, you are trying to see where the other person is coming from, not seeking a way in to explain how you feel. When a person feels fully heard, they feel less judgment.

Try to figure out what is motivating someone's fears. If you can understand why a person is acting a certain way, it's easier to not make assumptions or judgments.

Be curious and ask a lot of questions. It can make someone feel special and important if you show genuine interest in what's going on in her life.

Think about what is happening from someone else's perspective. This one is hard—and takes practice. But to be compassionate, it's important to really try to understand how another person sees a situation and not just rely on your own experience.

Most importantly, caring about anti-racism is a lifelong journey, and not everyone begins that journey at the same time. Remember there was a time when you didn't know about anti-racism work or didn't care. That stage didn't define who you were. Judging others won't help them begin to care about racism. In fact, they might isolate themselves in their bubbles even more. Use your compassion to see the best in people, even when you don't agree.

creating community

Bringing people together who share anti-racist goals can be a fun—and powerful—way to learn and practice anti-racism.

A fun way to get started is by forming a book group with your friends. Ask your favorite teacher if she or he would be willing to sponsor and host a book club for an hour after school once a week. You could start with a book like this one to learn what motivates each of you to be an anti-racism activist and where you are in your understanding of race, racism, and being an ally. You could also read novels about people of color that will help you see things in a different way. This is a great step toward broadening your mind and experiencing life from a different racial perspective.

Here are some ideas for your book club:

Amina's Voice
By Hena Khan

Brown Girl Dreaming
By Jacqueline Woodson

Weedflower
By Cynthia Kadohata

Gaby, Lost and Found
By Angela Cervantes

Blended
By Sharon M. Draper

smart girls ★ American Girl
RACE & INCLUSION
standing up to racism and building a better world

With your teacher or a parent, search online for discussion guides for the books you choose. And then get reading—and talking.

Or consider starting a culture club to learn about different ethnic groups. Share books, movies, foods, and dances from various cultures. Set up field trips to museums and events that celebrate different backgrounds. You could even host a culture fair and ask people from your community to talk about their background and share pictures, clothing, stories, traditions, and food.

Of course, just going to a club after school will never make you an expert on diversity. But that's not the point. You're exploring other people's lives and experiences a little bit at a time. There will still be all kinds of racial experiences that you miss even after reading a novel or learning about other cultures. But these experiences give you ways to start seeing beyond your bubble.

anti-racism ideas at school

Sometimes our education gives us limited perspectives. Most history, literature, and social studies courses focus on White people, culture, and values, often overlooking the experiences of other groups. While the United States is a great country, it would be better if it confronted its legacy of racism, oppression, and violence. Facing the horrors of the past and the flaws of the present is key to creating a better future.

To prepare yourself and your classmates for a diverse world, work with teachers, school leaders, and school boards to improve your education. Ask for lessons that confront racism and celebrate diversity, and think about ways to expand the bubble in every type of class. Can you study Latin American history in greater detail? Can you ask to play music by Black composers in band class? Does art class expose you to enough artists of color and their art?

Some people will think these changes are unnecessary or disruptive. Ask them to think about all the people and stories that are left out of your schoolbooks. Explain that you want to experience the diversity of cultures in the world. Colleges and employers want students who are good at math, science, and writing. But they also want students who are good people and who are knowledgeable about the world around them. Explain that in an increasingly diverse world, the best schools challenge students to think about anti-racism and what it means to be an ally.

go even bigger

Beyond the work you might do in your school, there are support networks you can create in and around your community. Perhaps your culture club friends are looking to make a new recipe or want to try learning Mandarin. You'll never run out of ways to expand your mind!

Or maybe your classmates aren't ready to join you in your anti-racism efforts. Remember how cozy and comfy the bubble can be? Not everyone wants to venture out, and you can't make anyone join you, even if your work is creating positive change. But school is just one place to start your learning journey. Branching out into your community will introduce you to all kinds of new people, experiences, and ideas.

Research cultural organizations in your town. Do they have cooking tutorials or dance classes? What about concerts, art classes, or discussion groups? Or maybe they have a cultural center you can visit. Check out schedules of events and pick a few you'd like to try. Attending public events can be a fun and powerful way to learn about different cultures.

Get creative! All these new experiences will give you new perspectives on how diverse and wonderful our world is. You will realize it's our differences that make us unique and beautiful.

volunteer

Pitching in to help community organizations further their anti-racism goals is a great way to practice anti-racism. It's exciting to think that your hard work will create big changes in our world, but little, everyday acts also make a difference. Groups that organize important activities and events like protests could also probably use volunteers to fold and mail newsletters or sort donations.

Research the needs of your community. Think about what skills you have to offer as well as how much time you have to give. Think about what you can do, what you should do, and what groups actually need you to do. Find the perfect blend of all three, and lend a hand!

Where to begin? Here are some ideas!

Hold a yard sale with neighbors and donate the money to a local anti-racism organization.

Give a school presentation about White privilege.

Write an article for your school newsletter about how to spot and stop microaggressions.

Make posters about discrimination to display at your school or library.

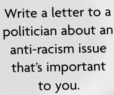

Write a letter to a politician about an anti-racism issue that's important to you.

Collect books that feature people of color and donate them to your library.

Buy goods and services from local businesses owned by people of color.

For your next birthday, ask friends and family to bring donations for a favorite anti-racism charity or cause.

Make crafts and sell them to raise money for a group that's fighting racism.

Attend a march dedicated to stopping racism.

If one or more of these sounds like you, give it a go! Big changes start with small steps.

feeling alone

Prepare for the possibility that people won't be as passionate as you are about anti-racism. Some people feel really comfortable and safe in their bubbles and want to stay there. Some fear that making the world better for others will make it worse for themselves. Some just might be too busy with other things to also take on fighting racism.

If people aren't ready, you can't make them care about the same issues you care about, no matter how hard you try. If you raise awareness, they might come around and start to wonder what fighting racism would mean for them. But don't spend too much time trying to convince someone to be on the same path as you. Spend your time focusing on what you can do to help the targets of racism. That's what's most important.

It can feel lonely trying to fight racism.

To help yourself stay dedicated, write down:

1. A goal you have for practicing anti-racism

2. The skills you use when you practice anti-racism

3. Why this work is important to you

It might look something like this:

1. I want people of color to feel valued for exactly who they are.

2. My writing skills help me share my opinions about anti-racism.

3. Helping to create a fairer society makes me feel proud and happy.

Look at this statement whenever you feel down to remind yourself what you're doing, why you're doing it, and who you're doing it for. Stay focused on the people you want to be an ally for—those who face racism every day.

Make sure you are doing anti-racism work because you want to create positive change, not to get recognition or awards. Anti-racism isn't a project you complete for a grade. You may not even hear the words "thank you" often. If your heart is in the right place, the change you see will be enough of a reward.

a lot to learn

There's so much to learn about anti-racism. It's easy to feel like you don't know enough. But you don't have to know everything. Nobody does! It's enough to know that you want to help and are dedicated to learning more.

Finding credible information is important. Talk to librarians and teachers, parents, or other trusted adults. Try to make this learning part of your schoolwork. If you have to write a biography for history, ask your teacher if you can do a report on a historically significant person of color. If you have to do a presentation about literature, ask if you can do one on Native American folktales. Combining learning about diversity with your school assignments is a great way to not only educate yourself but also enlighten your classmates and teachers along the way. It's critical that you don't rely on people of color to educate you. That's not their job. Use your smarts to track down resources that will educate you, and let your curiosity keep you moving forward.

Admitting you're not an expert is an important first step in anti-racism work. Sometimes people who think they know everything don't listen when they are wrong. They might say insulting things, or hold back and even harm the same groups they say they want to help. Instead, spend more time listening than talking, and don't assume that you have the solutions. Stay humble and ask how you can help make a difference.

STAY CURIOUS AND KEEP WORKING

If racism pushes people of color aside, make sure your anti-racism invites and makes room for them at the center.

finding balance

There's no doubt that anti-racism work will take a lot of your time and energy. As you grow up, you're going to have other passions and goals that will also become a big part of who you are. If you focus too much on any one thing, you can burn out and fail to accomplish anything at all. So your anti-racism efforts have to energize you, too.

Find ways to incorporate anti-racism work into your daily life. Just like you can bring anti-racism topics into your schoolwork, you can combine them with the things you do for fun.

Those who commit to anti-racism find ways to maintain balance, and those who achieve balance are those who figure out how to blend these issues into their every-day lives.

For example, Madison and Selah can combine their participation in the Drama Club with their interest in stopping bigotry by performing plays that deal with social justice issues.

NO MORE BIGOTRY

Starring Madison + Selah

BAXLEY THEATER

What are some ways you can stay energized in your anti-racism work? Write some ideas down and talk them over with others in your anti-racism community. Hearing how others stay balanced might give you some new ideas!

take care of you

When you're an ally, anti-racism work can feel exhausting, so make sure you take a break when you need to. To help others, you have to care for yourself. Many people of color experience racism every single day. They can't take a rest from daily situations that are unjust and hurtful. That's why it's important for you to take a break, reset, and then get back at it!

If you're a person of color practicing anti-racism, you might feel extra tired. It's hard to deal with ongoing racism *and* fight it day after day. It's especially important to listen to your body and give it the rest it needs.

This is hard work, and you might get discouraged, frustrated, or sad. Think about what you do to de-stress, such as going for a walk, cuddling with a pet, or watching a funny movie with a friend. Make a list of those self-care ideas and go back to it when you need a pick-me-up.

If you take a break and try to reset but you just can't, it's time to ask for help. Whether it's checking in with other girls who are doing this work or talking to a trusted adult, it's important to talk about your feelings. Other people can help you stay on track and give you the tools to keep going. Lean on each other!

SELF-CARE

Shoot hoops with Imani.

Help Dad in the garden.

Daydream under the tree in the backyard.

Make a playlist of my favorite songs. Sing loudly!

Take Dexter for a walk.

Video chat with Nana.

If you're feeling burned out, reenergize by thinking back to how you first started doing this work. Watching a movie about an inspiring person who persisted through tough times could give you the boost you need to keep going. When you're celebrating diversity, you're seeing the positive actions of your anti-racism work. Balance the hard work with the rewarding fun to keep your spirits up!

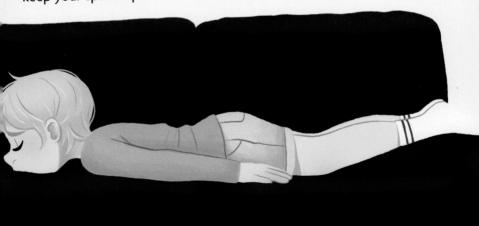

anti-racism checklist

Standing up to racism is a lifelong commitment. Use this checklist to remain motivated, engaged, and energized by your hard work and to keep track of your progress.

☐ Finish all the mini-challenges on page 39.

☐ Write a new set of mini-challenges for yourself.

☐ Share your knowledge, and make a mini-challenge list for your friends and your family!

☐ Reach out to people who have a different understanding of anti-racism and practice listening with compassion.

☐ Write a script of what you might say if you saw racist behavior at school.

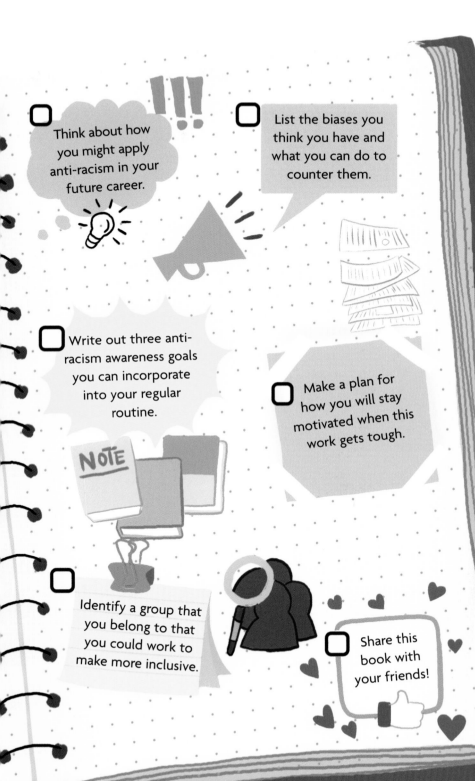

☐ Think about how you might apply anti-racism in your future career.

☐ List the biases you think you have and what you can do to counter them.

☐ Write out three anti-racism awareness goals you can incorporate into your regular routine.

☐ Make a plan for how you will stay motivated when this work gets tough.

☐ Identify a group that you belong to that you could work to make more inclusive.

☐ Share this book with your friends!

promise of the future

What's YOUR commitment to anti-racism?

To continue to grow, you have to make a commitment. A lot of things compete for our attention and time, but if you promise to keep learning and pushing yourself outside your comfort zone, then you are much more likely to stay true to the ideas of anti-racism.

Remember the bubbles in your world? Think about the influence you have in your bubbles. What are your unique skills within your bubbles, and how can you use those skills to improve racial fairness? What anti-racist actions can you make a commitment to?

Write down a pact that you can look at when you need inspiration or energy to carry on with your anti-racism work. Here's an example to get you started.

Make it happen

I commit to sharing my anti-racism knowledge with

_____.

Three anti-racism ideas I can share with a friend:

1 _____

2 _____

3 _____

I promise to use my skills of _____
to create positive, anti-racist change.

In my circle of _____, I'll use my influence
to change _____.

I commit to these anti-racism actions:

_____

_____

_____

_____

Come back here often to see how you're doing. Do you need to make a
new commitment? Do you need help with another? Reach out to your
friends, family, and community for support. If we all make these types of
commitments, we can all enjoy a fairer, more just world. Let's go!

About the Author

Deanna Singh is an accomplished author, educator, business leader, and champion for marginalized communities. As the founder and Chief Change Agent of Flying Elephant, a holding company for multiple social enterprises, Deanna consults with individuals and companies that are looking to make a positive difference in the world. She is known for giving clients the tools and courage to imagine, activate, and impact the world as agents of change. She is also the author of other children's and business books. Singh earned a BA in urban studies from Fordham University, a JD from Georgetown University, an MBA from the University of Wisconsin–Madison, and a certificate in diversity, equity, and inclusion from Cornell.

About the Illustrator

Shellene Rodney is a Toronto-based illustrator with a passion for illustrating experiences and emotions through the various stages of life. Her characters are often closely tied to personal experience. From the time she was a small child, she was influenced by the art around her, which helped build her understanding about art and creativity. Illustration and storytelling are among the many avenues that she uses to express her own unique ideas. Youth, children, and adventurous adults are her favorite subjects!

About the Advisers

Traci Baxley, EdD, is a professor of multicultural education and curriculum and instruction at Florida Atlantic University. She's a mother of five, consultant, educator, and coach dedicated to supporting families, organizations, and corporations in developing inclusive practices that lead to meaningful relationships, genuine belonging, and high productivity. She is also the creator of Social Justice Parenting®, a philosophy that moves families from fear-based parenting to parenting from a place of radical love—through compassion and social justice engagement.

Deborah Rivas-Drake, PhD, is a professor of education and psychology at the University of Michigan. The overarching goal of her work is to illuminate promising practices that disrupt racism and xenophobia and help set diverse young people on trajectories of positive contribution to their schools and communities. In addition to academic publications, she has collaboratively developed materials for school leaders, district policy makers, and educators and writings and webinars for parents and educators.

Tell us about your anti-racism journey.

Write to us!
Race & Inclusion Editor
American Girl
8400 Fairway Place
Middleton, WI 53562

Here are some other American Girl books you might like:

Each sold separately. Find more books online at americangirl.com.

Parents, request a FREE catalog at **americangirl.com/catalog**.
Sign up at **americangirl.com/email** to receive the latest news and exclusive offers.

americangirl.com/play